Come, Let Me Tell You About The Crypto Election Project!

A Crypto Project Built By One Of The People, For The People

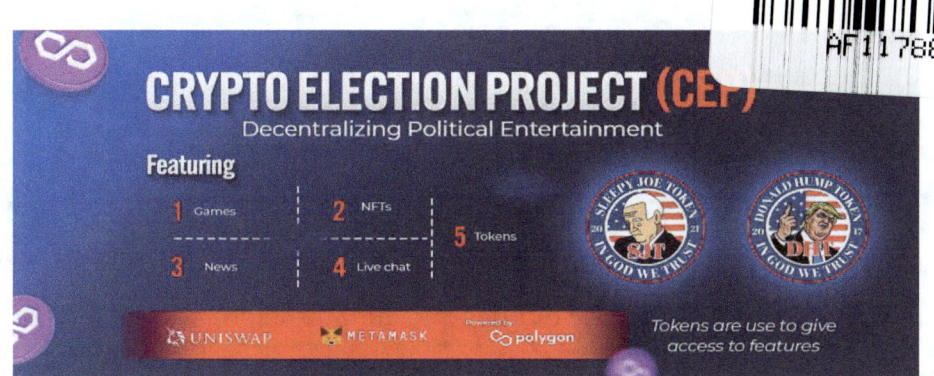

An Innovative Ideas, LLC. Project

Michael McNaught

Are you Interested in learning about Cryptocurrency (Crypto) and Blockchain Technology? Would you like to interact with a live crypto project with a guided tour?

Well, look no further. This is the book for you!

Copyright

Come, Let Me Tell You About The Crypto Election Project!
A CryptoProject Built By One Of The People, For The People

Written By Michael McNaught

Copyright © 2025 Crypto Election Project (CEP). An Innovative Ideas, LLC. project.

All Rights Reserved.

This book or any portions thereof may not be reproduced or used in any manner whatsoever without the expressed written permission of the publisher except for the use of brief quotation in a book review.

Disclaimer:
- This book is exclusively for educational purposes. Any financial decisions made by you, are at your own risk.
- The Crypto Election Project was created for entertainment purposes only. This project is not affiliated or endorsed by any political parties or any member of a political party.

Preface

Hi, My Name Is Michael McNaught, A Bioanalytical Scientist by profession and an avid crypto enthusiast. A lot of crypto projects are anonymously owned and operated. This project isn't. Yes, I am the mastermind behind this awesome Crypto project. Thank you for your interest in my project.

The Crypto Election Project was designed and built to be a fun, exciting, and engaging crypto project based off of the 2024 Presidential Election. This unique project was built with crypto novices in mind. Therefore, everything was carefully designed and built for simplicity and ease of use to enhance the user's experience.

In this guide, I will try my very best to make things very simple and easy to understand. It'll be fun working your way through these pages and getting to try stuff out in realtime. But if you would like to have a comprehensive theoretical understanding of Cryptocurrency and Blockchain Technology, meaning, you would like to understanding all the fancy crypto terms, acronyms, and complicated jargons that the crypto nerds keep tossing around, please check out my other book 'Cryptocurrency Chronicles; Unlocking the secrets of blockchain technology.' In that book, I explain everything you need to know, as far as cryptocurrency and blockchain technology is concerned. Anyhow, in this book, we'll only be focusing on the Crypto Election Project. Let's dive in!

Table Of Content

Introduction 1

The Crypto Election Project (CEP) 3

A Full tour of the CEP Website 4

Home Page 5

Features 14

Game Gallery Page 15

NFTs Gallery Page 20

News Feed Page 26

Live Chat 28

Tokens 30

Polygon Blockchain: An Overview 32

Vote For The Crypto Election Project 38

Join Our Social Media Groups 41

Contact US 43

Introduction

The story behind the Crypto Election Project (CEP).

I actually came up with the idea for CEP while at work joking around with co-workers about the funny name calling between Donoald Trump and Joe Biden. Donald Trump gave Joe Biden the name Sleep Joe and Joe Biden called Donalod Trump, Donald Hump. Its there on Youtube, go check! I'm still not sure if that was just a slip of the tongue for Mr. Biden or if it was actually intentional. We may never know. Anyhow, I found it to be really funny. I thought that these names were really humorous and that they actually fit their personalities. Mr. Biden always looks discombobulated and like he's ready to take a nap, and Mr. Trump always seems to be getting himself into trouble with the ladies. Based on this, I thought "you know what, this might actually make a really great idea for a crypto themed election memecoin project." Thus CEP was borned.

I really wanted to build something that was unique, engaging and fun; something different from what was already on the market. So I kept coming up with crazy/unique ideas on different elements that I could incorporate into the project that would set it apart from other memecoin projects.

All those ideas culminated into what the project is today. And I must say, I'm pretty pleased with my efforts in creating something truly unique. This is actually the first time I've ever built a project of this magnitude and scale. Boy, was it a lot of work. I really did learn a lot though, through this experience. On this project, I got to work with some really talented and awesome blockchain developers, website developers, game developers, NTF designers, etc. Learning new skills can actually be fun, exciting, and rewarding.

All my ideas that I have developed into either a product or a project, are housed under my registered business, Innovative Ideas, LLC.

The long term goal of this project is that around every four years, coinciding with the US election cycle, the project will be updated with additional tokens and features that match the current election. I believe that this project has great potential and could be the next big thing in crypto, so I'm hoping that I will get the full support of the crypto community. Let's make the Crypto Election Project the next Shiba Inu or Pepe!

The Crypto Election Project (CEP)

Let me now give you an overview of the Crypto Election Project (CEP). CEP is an election themed memecoin crypto project built on the Polygon blockchain. The project uses the POL token for on-chain transactions. The project features two tokens [Sleepy Joe Token (SJT) and Donald Hump Token (DHT)], a game gallery, an NFT gallery, a news feed page, and a live chat page. The SJT and DHT tokens can be swapped on Uniswap for the POL token, and vice versa. The two tokens are used to grant access to the web3 games on the game gallery. They are also used to grant a discount to project members when purchasing NFTs from the NFT gallery. Your tokens will never be used or depleted, unless sold, they are only used to verify that you are a member of the CEP project. You are a member of the project if you hold either SJT or DHT in your crypto wallet. MetaMask is the crypto wallet of choice for this project.

Currently, the games in the game gallery are only optimized for Desktop and Laptop use. I'll now give you a guided tour of the project's website and the project's features.

A Full tour of the CEP Website

Note: all the website images below have been zoomed to -50 within the browser. This was done for presentation purposes. So when you visit the website, your images will be set to 100%, your browser's default.

Home Page

https://cryptoelectionproject.tech/

The home page website of the project displays all the information you need to do your own research on the project. Always **DO YOUR OWN RESEARCH** (DYOR). This cannot be overstated. This project is fully transparent, therefore no information that you need to do a comprehensive research has been hidden or concealed. The project token contracts have also been renounced so no further alterations can be made to them. Another important information is that the Liquidity Pool (LP) tokens have been locked for 5 years. All this information and much more is available on the project's home page.

As I have mentioned previously, I built this project with crypto novices in mind so I have meticulously provided all the information, details, and resources needed on how to get set-up, if you wish to participate in the project. That is, setting-up your MetaMask wallet, connecting it to the Polygon network, and funding your wallet with POL tokens to conduct on-chain transactions. Everything you need is on the project's website.

A lot of thought went into designing a clean and fully functional website with all the necessary resources at your fingertips, without making the page too cluttered. There is a lot to explore and learn on the website's home page. You can also check out the Polygon block explorer, Polygonscan. This is a very useful blockchain tool used to check all on-chain transactions conducted on the Polygon network.

Image #1

Image #1. On this section of the website we have the following:
- A bar at the top showing the current price for Bitcoin, Ethereum, and the POL token.
- A running advertisement banner for businesses interested in advertising with us.
- The project's social media accounts [Telegram, and Discord] were our project's community members hangout.
- Buttons which directs you to our various Feature pages [Game Gallery, NFT Gallery, News Feed page, Live Chat page].
- Buy/Sell buttons which directs you to the token's Uniswap Buy/Sell page.

- A button which directs you to the 'How to BuY' section of the website.
- A Decentralized Exchange (DEX) analytics tool button which directs you to GeckoTerminal, a very useful CoinGecko tool. You just need to search for either **SJT** or **DHT** in the website's search bar.
    - GeckoTerminal is a platform that allows users to track real-time crypto prices, trading volume, transactions, liquidity, and more on decentralized exchanges across all blockchain.

Image #2

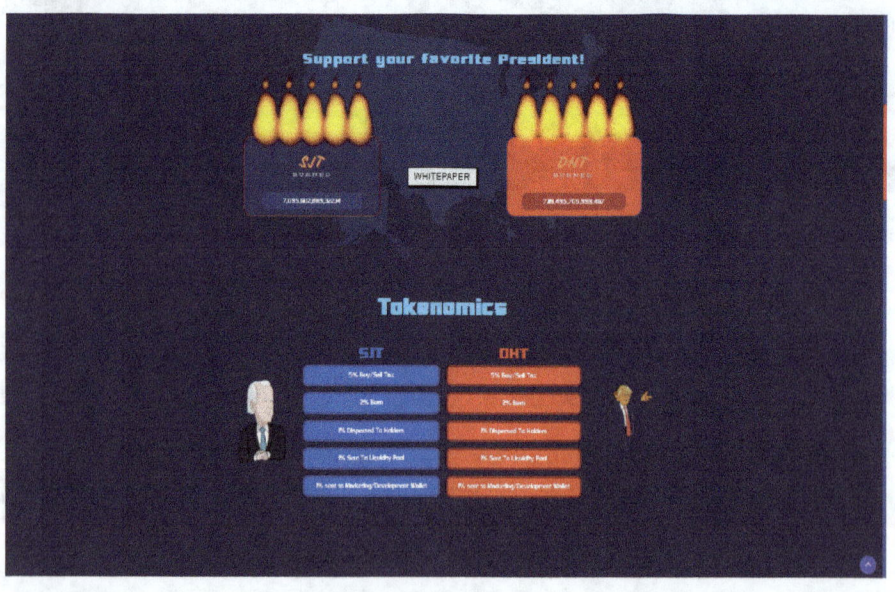

Image #2. On this section of the website we have the following:
- The SJT and DHT burn tracker. These are updated in real-time with every SJT or DHT buy/sell transactions.

- The tokenomics section which shows the economic aspect of the project, its token distributions and allocations.

Image #3

Image #3. On this section of the website we have the following:
- The 'How To Buy' section. This section has six (6) easy, clear and concise steps on how to set-up your MetaMask wallet, how to fund it with POL tokens, and how to purchase your SJT or DHT tokens on Uniswap. I tried to give additional resources in case it's needed, so ALL **blue** text in this section are clickable links which bring you to web pages with relevant information.
    - Note: no single wallet, except the project's Marketing/Development wallet, can hold more than 5% of the token's total supply. This was coded in the token's smart contracts and was implemented to prevent whales from hoarding a large amount of the token's total supply.

- 'Set Up Tutorial' by clicking this link, you will be directed to the project's Youtube page where I have compiled a video playlist which also walks you through the set-up process.

Image #4

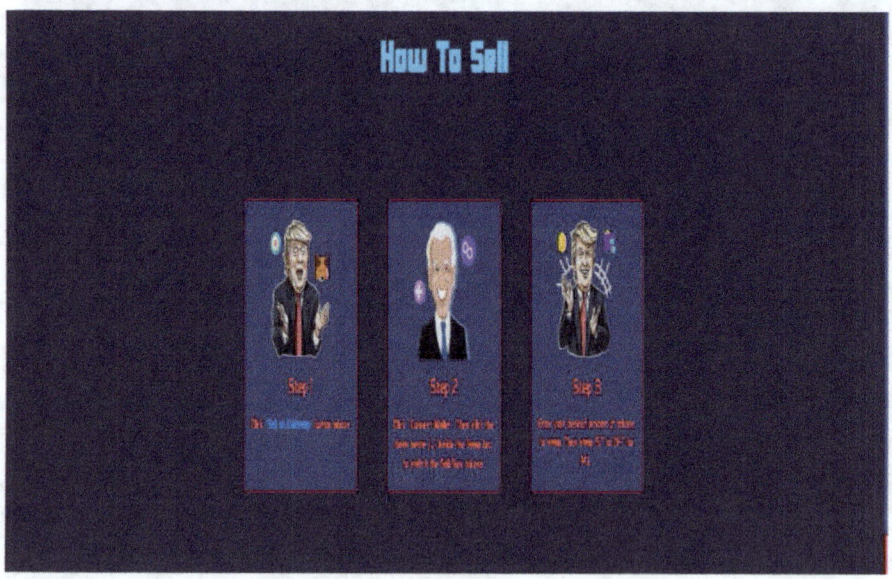

Image #4. On this section of the website we have the following:
- The 'How To Sell' section. This section has three (3) easy, clear and concise steps on how to sell your SJT or DHT tokens on Uniswap. On Uniswap you'll swap your SJT or DHT tokens back to the POL token, at which point you can either swap to another token, or cashout to fiat through a centralized exchange (CEX) like Coinbase, Crypto.com, etc. The text in blue in this section redirects you to the sell button on the website.

Image #5

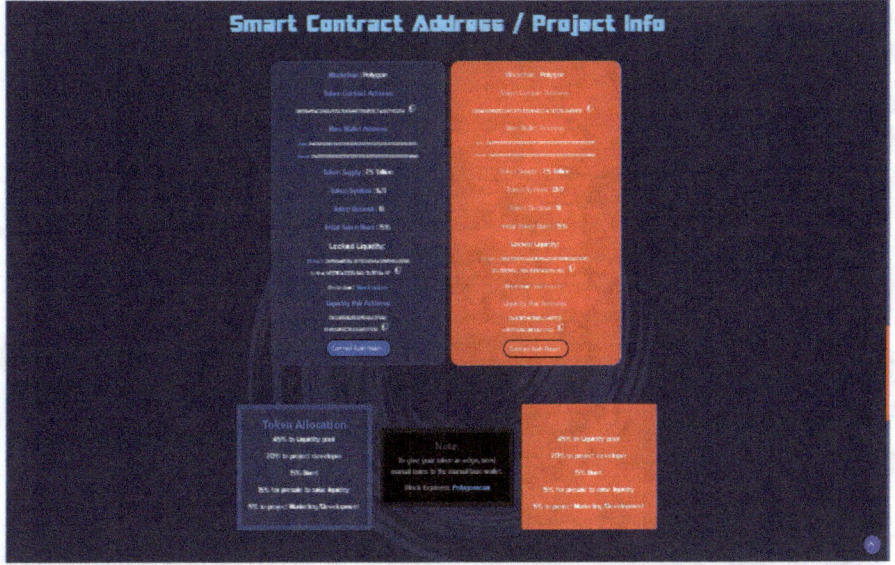

Image #5. On this section of the website we have the following:
- 'Smart Contract Address/ Project Info.' Here you'll find all the project's smart contract information, including tokens contract address, burn wallet address, liquidity lock information, smart contracts audit report, etc. This section provides vital information for DYOR.
    - Note: there are a few clickable links in this section, as well as copy buttons for easy address copying.
- This section also shows the initial token allocations. That is, how much tokens were initially burnt, used to create the liquidity pool, allocated to marking, etc.
- In the 'Note' section, we've included a link [blue text] that directs you to the Polygon Block Explorer, Polygonscan.
    - A Blockchain Explorer is an online tool that enables you to search for real-time and historical information about a

blockchain, including data related to blocks, transactions, addresses, and more.

Image #6

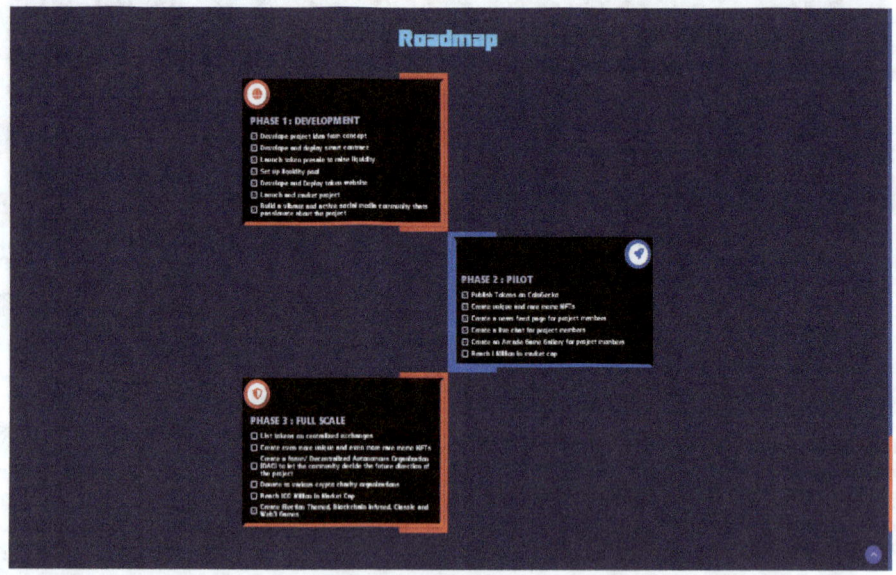

Image #6. On this section of the website we have the following:

- 'Roadmap.' This section displays our goals for the project. As we accomplish our goals through each phase of the project, they are checked off from our list. As you can see, we have already accomplished quite a bit from our lofty and ambitious plans. We intend to fulfill ALL the set goals from our list.

Image #7

Image #7. This is the end of the homepage.

Here we have the following:
- Buy buttons, which again directs you to Uniswap for token purchasing.
- How to Buy button, which directs you to the relevant section of the homepage.

Image #8

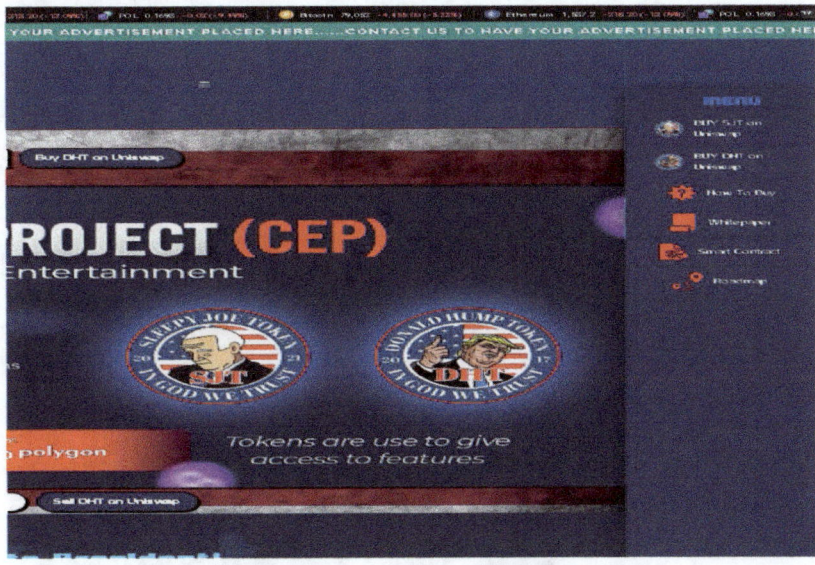

Image #8. By clicking on the menu button ▬, the menu to the right in image #8 pops out. You can access the Buy buttons, the 'How To Buy'

section of the page, the Whitepaper, and the smart contract information section of the page, from this pop out menu.

On each page of the website you'll see this button . Clicking this Button brings you back to the top of the page.

Features

The Crypto Election Project has five (5) elements I've called Features. They are as follows:
1. Game Gallery
2. NFTs Gallery
3. New Feed page
4. Live Chat page
5. Tokens [SJT & DHT]
    - Note: Tokens are used to grant access to the web3 games. They are also used to grant project members a discount when purchasing NFTs from the NFTs Gallery. You are considered a project member if you hold either SJT or DHT in your crypto wallet.

Now let's explore each of the Features mentioned above in more detail.

Game Gallery Page

https://gamegallery.cryptoelectionproject.tech/

Currently, the project's game gallery houses six (6) games; three (3) 2D games and three (3) web3 games. All the games were built from the ground up specifically for the project. The 2D games are free to play by anyone. However, the web3 games are only accessible to project members. That is, you have to hold either SJT or DHT in your crypto wallet in order to play. Any amount of SJT or DHT valuing ~$5 USD or more will grant you access. (note: your tokens are **NOT** used up and will never be depleted, they are only used to verify project membership and to grant access).

Please be aware that the games on the game gallery are optimized for Desktop and Laptop game playing. They are not optimized for mobile devices.

Games:
2D games [PAC-MAN, Snake, Tetris]
- All popular classic single player games, all U.S. election themed.

Web3 games [Pool, Air Hockey, Red Light (Squid Game)]
- To play the web3 games, you'll first need to connect your crypto wallet which has either SJT or DHT in it. The token has to be visible to your wallet's user interface (UI).

All these games can be played in either single or multiplayer mode

- Pool- 2 players in multiplayer mode
- Air Hockey- 2 players in multiplayer mode
- Red Light- up to 10 players in multiplayer mode

In multiplayer mode (which I also call 'Betting Mode'), a bet has to be made between each player, and in-game coins have to be purchased with POL tokens. 1 in-game coin = 5 POL tokens. The winner of the game will claim 90% of the bet pool and the Crypto Election Project gets 10%. That is, if you bet 1 in-game coin and the other player bets 1 in-game coin, the winner will receive 90% of the sum of the 2 coins. Therefore, the winner would receive 1.80 in-game coin and the CEP project would receive 0.2 in-game coin. At the end of each game you can cashout your coins back to the POL token.

There is only a minimum bet limit of 1 in-game coin. There is no bet maximum limit. For the Red Light game which can host up to 10 players at the same time, 90% of the bet pool sum would be 9 in-game coins, which would be claimed by the winner of that game. The project would receive 1 in-game coin from the pool of 10 in-game coins, that is, if 1 coin is bet by each 10 players.

- The web3 games All have in-game chat when in multiplayer mode, so each player can communicate with each other.
- Your purchased NFTs from the NFTs gallery can be used as your Avatar profile picture in each of the web3 games.

Image #9

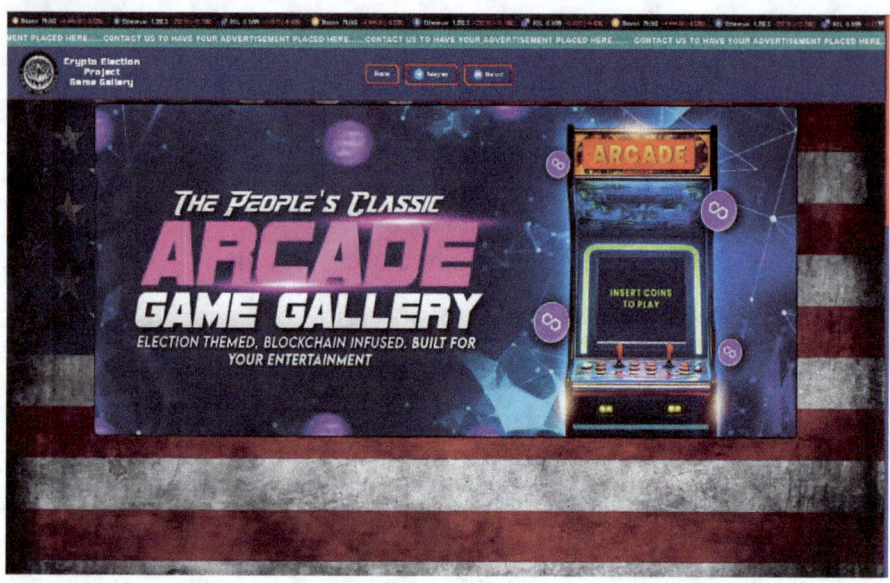

Image #9. On this section of the website we have the following:
- The Crypto price banner at the top of the page (previously discussed).
- The advertisement banner (previously discussed).
- The project's social media accounts (previously discussed).
- A home button which directs you back to the project's homepage.

Image #10

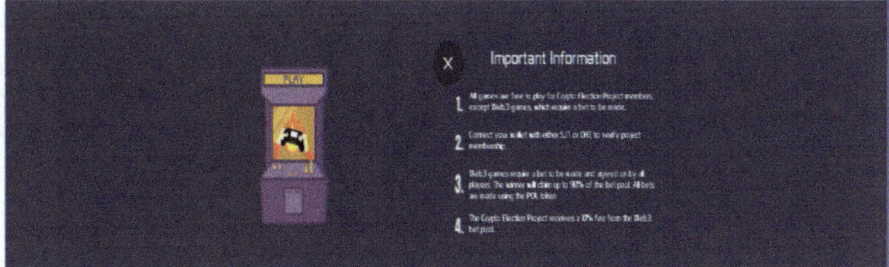

Image #10. On this section of the website we have the following:

- An 'Important Information' section. Please read this section carefully, especially information pertaining to the web3 games and its betting multiplayer mode.

Image #11

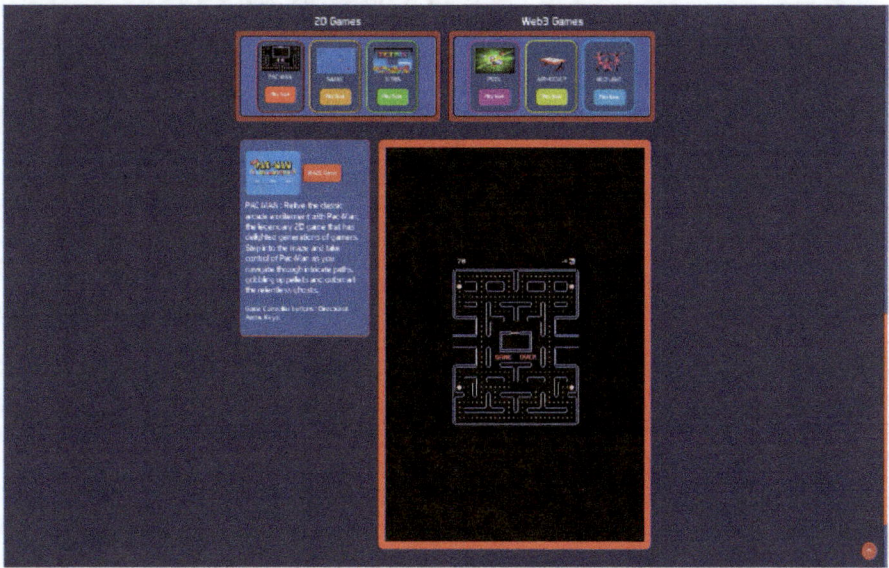

Image #11. On this section of the website we have the following:

- The game selection Icons

- Clicking on the game icons in either the 2D game section or the web3 game section, changes the game screen to the selected game.

- The Game information box
    - This section gives an introduction to the game selected, and it also displays relevant information for game playing, such as, game control keys, game functions, web3 game smart contracts, etc.

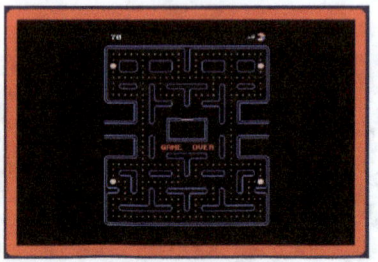

- The Game play screen
    - This is the game playing area. You can increase or decrease your browser zoom or use your browser Full screen mode for the best game playing experience. The web3 games have an expansion button which can be clicked.

NFTs Gallery Page

https://nftgallery.cryptoelectionproject.tech/

The project's NFT Gallery has over 17000 unique NFT images of US Presidents and Vice President. Each image has unique traits and are in limited amounts. NFTs can be purchased by anyone, but if you are a project member, you'll receive an automatic 10% discount upon minting your NFTs.

NFTs that have been purchased from the NFT galley, that are in your connected crypto wallet, can be used as your in-game profile avatars for the web3 games. You can also list your NFTs on an NFT exchange, such as OpenSea, for resale or trading.

Note:
- For NFT purchasing you'll need to fund your crypto walled with POL tokens. NFTs are swapped for POL tokens.
- No single wallet can hold more than a specified amount of NFTs from a single NFT collection, (See NFT gallery page). This was done to prevent Whales from hoarding too many NFTs.

Image #12

Image #12. On this section of the NFT gallery website we have the following:

- The Crypto price banner at the top of the page (previously discussed).
- The advertisement banner (previously discussed).
- The project's social media accounts (previously discussed).
- A home button which directs you back to the project's homepage.
- A wallet connect button for connecting your MetaMask wallet to conduct on-chain transactions.

Image #13

Image #13. On this section of the website we have the following:

- The NFT contract address. After you purchase your NFTs, you'll need to add the contract address to your crypto wallet to make the NFT visible to your wallet user UI. Clear and concise steps are given in the "How To Mint NFTs' section of the website. Clicking the copy button 🗐, copies the NFT smart contract address.

- Here we also have the NFT transaction window

By clicking on the images to the left, the box will be highlighted and the window to the right will switch to the selected NFT collection. Here you'll also find the NFT price and mint max amount per wallet.

Image #14

Image #14. On this section of the website we have the following:
- 'Important Information.' This section contains information that you need to know. Please read carefully.

Note:
- There is a 2.5% royalty that is affixed to the resale of each NFT purchase from the project's NFT gallery. This means that it was coded into the NFT smart contract that each time the NFT is resold, a 2.5% of the sold price is automatically paid to the project's Marketing/Development wallet.

Image #15

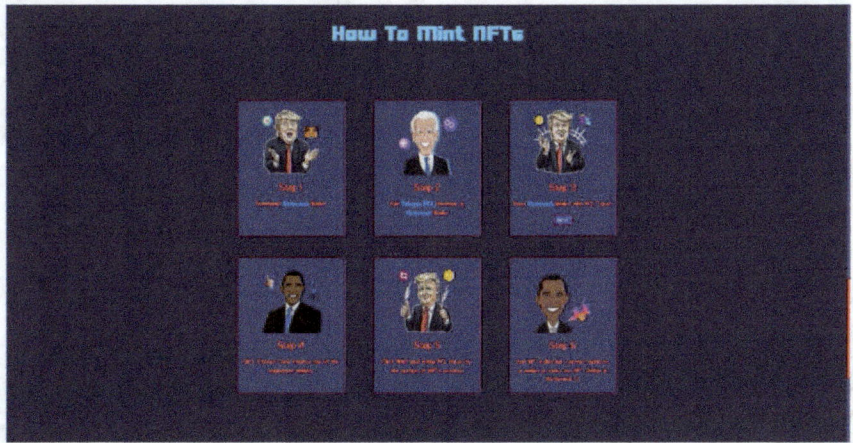

Image #15. On this section of the website we have the following:
- 'How To Mint NFTS.' Here I provided six (6) clear, concise, and easy steps on how to mint your NFTs from the project's NFT gallery. Remember, text in blue are clickable links which provide additional information and instructions.

Image #16

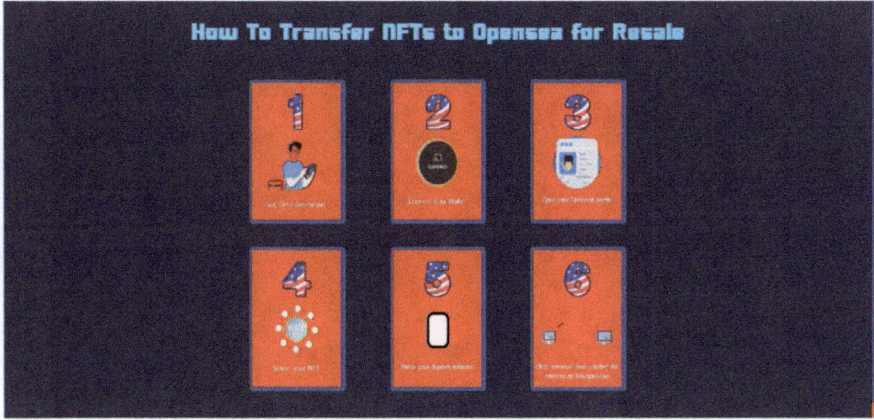

Image #16. On this section of the website we have the following:
- 'How To transfer NFTs to OpenSea for resale.' Here, I again provide you with six (6) easy, clear and concise steps on how to resell your NFTs on an NFT exchange platform. OpenSea is one of the most popular platforms for NFT resale and trading.

Image #17

Image #17. At the end of the NFT Gallery website we have the following:
- A link (blue Text) which directs you to an OpenSea article which provides you additional information about the OpenSea platform and how to sell an NFT on OpenSea. This link provides very useful information. You should definitely check it out.

News Feed Page

https://news.cryptoelectionproject.tech/

The News Feed page displays the latest political news, technology news, cryptocurrency news, web3 news, and NFT news. All news articles are continuously being refreshed several times per day. You should definitely check it out for your latest and most up to date news forecast. Did I mention that it's FREE? Well, the project covers the expenses for this service. Another awesome Feature of the Crypto Election Project.

Image #18

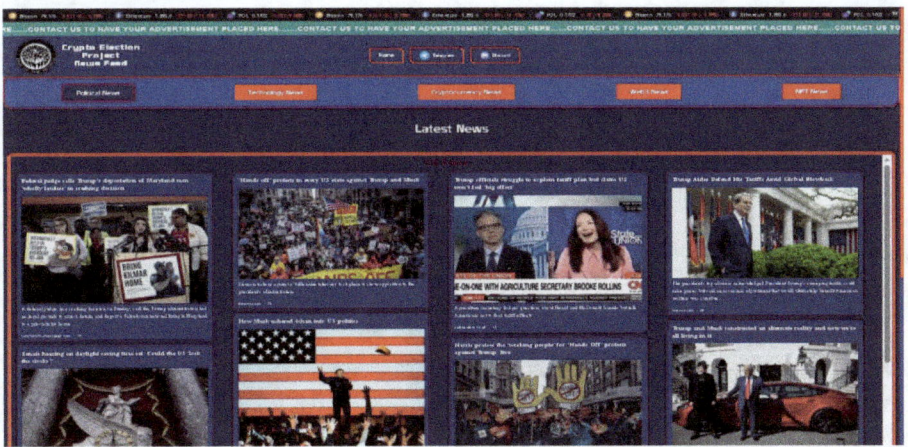

Image #18. On this section of the News Feed page website we have the following:

- The Crypto price banner at the top of the page (previously discussed).

26

- The advertisement banner (previously discussed).
- The project's social media accounts (previously discussed).
- A home button which directs you back to the project's homepage.
- The News Feed category selection buttons

Clicking any one of these buttons will change the window below the bar to the respective news feed. Clicking on the new heading in the news box will direct you to the respective offsite page with the news article or news video.

Live Chat

https://chat.cryptoelectionproject.tech/

The Live Chat is a pretty cool feature for a crypto project. As far as I am aware, the Crypto Election Project is the first memecoin project to implement this decentralized chat technology powered by Chitchatter. Anyone logged into the Live Chat website, is able to communicate live through either text, audio, or video. All communications are encrypted through blockchain decentralized technology. Check it out, it's really awesome! And did I mention that it's also FREE?

Image #19

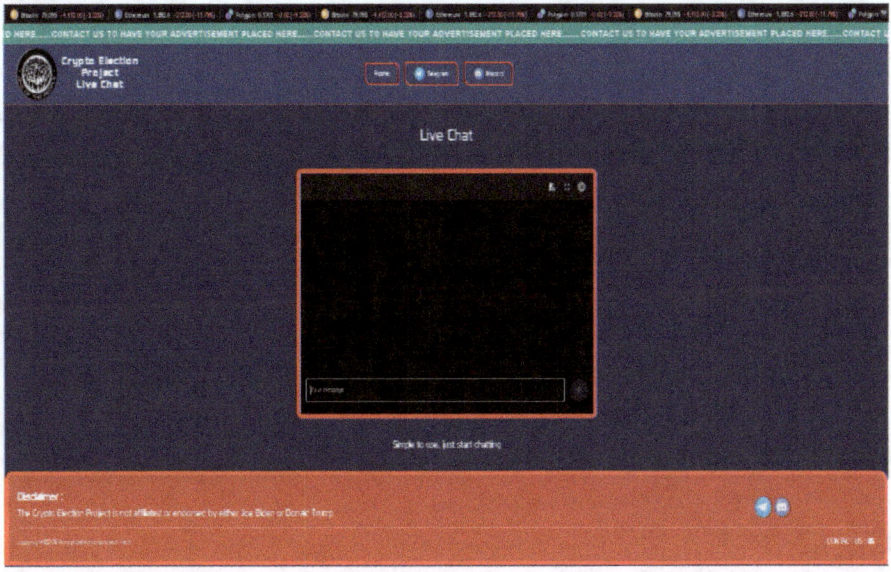

Image #19. On this section of the Live Chat page website we have the following:

- The Crypto price banner at the top of the page (previously discussed).
- The advertisement banner (previously discussed).
- The project's social media accounts (previously discussed).
- A home button which directs you back to the project's homepage.
- The 'Live Chat' window. This window will display your text, audio, or video chats. You can do screen sharing, and you can also share files with whoever you are chatting to. You can even do group chats as well.

Tokens

Sleepy Joe Token [SJT] & Donald Hump Token [DHT]

As mentioned in previous sections, the SJT and DHT tokens are used to grant access to the web3 games on the game gallery, and they are also used to grant a discount to NFT buyers who are project members. The tokens in your crypto wallet will never be used up during the two cases mentioned above.

However, through token trading, that is the buying or selling of SJT or DHT tokens, there is a 5% Buy/Sell tax that is incurred upon each transaction. The 5% tax is distributed as follows:
- 2% is burnt.
- 1% is dispersed to the crypto wallet of project members.
- 1% is sent to the Uniswap liquidity pool.
- 1% is sent to the project's Marking/Development crypto wallet.

There is a total token supply of 25 Trillion with an initial burn of 15% of the total supply. The current amount of tokens that's burnt so far is displayed in realtime on the project's homepage. 45% of the token's total supply was used to set up the liquidity pool on Uniswap. The token's liquidity LP token has been locked for a period of 5 years and expires on 13Aug2029. The ownership for the smart contrasts for each token has been renounced. Therefore, the developers of this project are no longer able to make any changes or alterations to the token's contracts. All information needed to do your own research is displayed on the project's homepage. **Please do your own research!**

Besides the project's maintenance and operation cost, the idea behind the token tax is to use it as a deterrent to early token dumping. The goal is that as the project's token supply is burnt, as the project increases in popularity, and as the project membership grows, the tokens you hold will steadily increase in value over time. Well, that's the hope!

Polygon Blockchain: An Overview

Polygon is a Layer 2 scaling solution designed to enhance the performance of Ethereum by offering faster transactions, lower fees, and improved scalability. Originally launched as Matic Network in 2017, it was later rebranded to Polygon in 2021, evolving into a multi-chain ecosystem that supports a wide range of scaling solutions.

1. What is Polygon?

Polygon is a protocol and framework for building and connecting Ethereum-compatible blockchain networks. It enables developers to create scalable, user-friendly dApps (decentralized applications) with high throughput and low transaction costs.

It functions as a sidechain to Ethereum, meaning it processes transactions separately and periodically submits a summary to the Ethereum mainnet. This significantly reduces congestion and lowers gas fees while maintaining Ethereum's security.

2. Key Features of Polygon

a) Scalability

- Uses sidechains, rollups, and other scaling techniques to process transactions more efficiently.

- Increases Ethereum's transaction speed from ~15 TPS to thousands of TPS (transactions per second).

b) Low Transaction Fees

- Gas fees on Polygon are a fraction of a cent, compared to Ethereum's often high costs.

- This makes it ideal for DeFi, gaming, and NFT projects that require frequent transactions.

c) Ethereum Compatibility

- Fully compatible with Ethereum smart contracts, tools, and dApps.

- Developers can migrate Ethereum-based projects to Polygon with minimal changes.

d) Security

- Uses Ethereum's security through the Polygon PoS (Proof-of-Stake) consensus mechanism.

- Also supports Zero-Knowledge (ZK) Rollups and other cryptographic security methods.

e) Multi-Chain Architecture

- Supports multiple blockchain infrastructures, such as:
    - Polygon PoS Chain – A Proof-of-Stake blockchain that runs alongside Ethereum.
    - Polygon zkEVM – Uses Zero-Knowledge Rollups to enhance Ethereum's security and efficiency.
    - Polygon Supernets – Custom blockchains for enterprises and specific use cases.

3. How Polygon Works

Polygon operates as a Layer 2 solution on top of Ethereum, meaning it processes transactions off-chain before committing them to Ethereum's mainnet. Here's how:

1. Users initiate transactions on Polygon.
2. Polygon validators process and confirm transactions quickly using the PoS consensus mechanism.
3. The finalized batch of transactions is sent back to Ethereum, ensuring security and transparency.

This hybrid approach reduces congestion on Ethereum, making it more efficient and cost-effective.

4. Use Cases of Polygon

Polygon's scalability and low fees make it suitable for a variety of blockchain applications:

a) DeFi (Decentralized Finance)

- Popular DeFi platforms like Aave, Uniswap, and Curve run on Polygon for cheaper transactions.
- Enables users to lend, borrow, and trade assets with minimal gas fees.

b) NFTs & Gaming

- OpenSea, Decentraland, and The Sandbox use Polygon for fast, low-cost NFT transactions.
- Many blockchain games (e.g., Zed Run, Aavegotchi) run on Polygon due to its low fees.

c) Web3 & Metaverse

- Supports metaverse projects like Decentraland and Somnium Space.
- Enables social applications, DAOs (Decentralized Autonomous Organizations), and decentralized identity solutions.

d) Enterprise & Custom Blockchains

- Polygon Supernets allow businesses to create custom blockchain networks tailored to specific needs.

- Governments and corporations can use Polygon ID for blockchain-based identity verification.

5. Polygon Token (POL)

POL is the native token of Polygon, used for:

- Transaction fees on the network.

- Staking to secure the PoS network.

- Governance, allowing users to vote on network upgrades.

POL has a fixed supply of 10 billion tokens and is widely used across the blockchain ecosystem.

6. Why Polygon Matters

Ethereum is the most popular blockchain for smart contracts, but its limitations (high fees, slow transactions) create barriers to mass adoption. Polygon solves these issues by providing:

- -Faster transactions
- -Lower costs
- -Ethereum compatibility
- -Flexible blockchain development

As Ethereum continues to evolve, Polygon plays a critical role in its future by providing scalable solutions for developers, businesses, and crypto users.

Vote For The Crypto Election Project

If you like the Crypto Election Project and you would like to see us thrive, show your support by voting for each token on the websites below. Just type **SJT** or **DHT** in the token search bar on the website, then select the token and vote by pressing the vote button. Every vote counts! Thank you in advance for your support.

Scan The QR code below:

1. **Top 100 Tokens**

    https://top100token.com/

2. **Coin Catapult**

   https://coincatapult.com/

3. **Gems Radar**

   https://gemsradar.com/

4. **Coinscope**

   https://www.coinscope.co/

Join Our Social Media Groups

If you would like to keep up with the Crypto Election Project, or if you would like to socialize with our vibrant and active crypto community, consider joining our social media groups below.

Scan the QR code below:

Telegram

https://t.me/cryptoelectionproject

Discord

https://discord.com/invite/3dZtGXfHdu

Contact US

For any questions, enquiries, comments, suggestions, partnerships, or business proposals, please reach out via the email address below, or through any of the contacts on our websites.

Scan the QR code below:

Innovative Ideas, LLC.
Email: mail@innovativeideas.tech
https://innovativeideas.tech/

Thank You For Supporting The Crypto Election Project!

Michael McNaught
One Of The People

HODL!

(hold on for dear life)

www.ingramcontent.com/pod-product-compliance
Lightning Source LLC
LaVergne TN
LVHW022001060526
838201LV00048B/1654